TAKING ACTION ON CLIMATE CHANGE

STARVED
Endangered Water and Food Supplies

ALEX DAVID

New York

Published in 2020 by Cavendish Square Publishing, LLC
243 5th Avenue, Suite 136, New York, NY 10016

First Edition

Website: cavendishsq.com

Cataloging-in-Publication Data
Names: David, Alex.
Title: Starved: endangered waters and food supplies / Alex David.
Description: New York : Cavendish Square, 2020. | Series: Taking action on climate change | Includes glossary and index.
Identifiers: ISBN 9781502652379 (pbk.) | ISBN 9781502652386 (library bound) | ISBN 9781502652393 (ebook)
Subjects: LCSH: Water-supply--Juvenile literature. | Water conservation--Juvenile literature. | Food-supply--Environmental aspects--Juvenile literature. | Sustainable agriculture--Juvenile literature.
Classification: LCC TD348.D38 2020 | DDC 628.1'62--dc23

Copy Editor: Nathan Heidelberger
Associate Art Director: Alan Sliwinski
Designer: Ginny Kemmerer
Production Coordinator: Karol Szymczuk
Photo Research: J8 Media

The photographs in this book are used by permission and through the courtesy of: Cover, Alohaflaminggo/Shutterstock.com; p. 4 Ellen Atkin/First Light/Getty Images; p. 8 Christian Petersen-Clausen/Moment/Getty Images; p. 10 Print Collector/Hulton Archive/Getty Images; p. 12 Steve Dunwell/Photolibrary/Getty Images; p. 14 © Minnesota Historical Society/Corbis/Getty Images; p. 16 ORLANDO SIERRA/AFP/Getty Images; p. 20 Green Stock Media/Alamy Stock Photo; p. 23 Katherine Frey/The Washington Post/Getty Images; p. 28 Peathegee Inc/Getty Images; p. 30 Kevin Trageser/The Image Bank/Getty Images; p. 33 Miksu, Own work/File: Global Seed Vault (cropped).jpg/Wikimedia Commons/CCA-SA 3.0 Unported; p. 36 Juliette Wade/Photolibrary/Getty Images; p. 38 Armin Weigel/dpa/Alamy Stock Photo; p. 41 ANGELA WEISS/AFP/Getty Images; p. 43 Neil Overy/Gallo Images/Getty Images; p. 45 DooFi, Own work/File: Cloud Seeding.svg/Wikimedia Commons/Public Domain; p. 46 TPG/Getty Images; p. 48 ralucahphotography.ro/Moment/Getty Images; p. 50 Mny-Jhee/Shutterstock.com; p. 51 Sibadon/Shutterstock.com; p. 54 Akif Patel/EyeEm/Getty Images.

Printed in the United States of America

Portions of this book originally appeared in *Safeguarding Water and Food Supplies* by Janet Craig.

CONTENTS

An organic farm in British Columbia, Canada, grows biodiverse lettuce in its rich soil.

Introduction

Forty-five minutes from Sioux Falls, South Dakota, sits an unassuming farm called Berrybrook Organics. However, this farm is something of a revolution. Farmers Will and Sherilyn Ortman, along with their three children, believe that soil is essential to good farming. According to Will Ortman, "Everything that we eat comes off of the soil, originally, and the soil is a living organism." The Ortmans do everything they can to farm in a way that cares for their soil.

Since the Industrial Revolution, our climate has been changing. Rain fluctuates. Sometimes it is very dry. Sometimes it is very wet. We live in a world of heat waves and floods. This does not make life for farmers easy, and therefore our food supply suffers.

Knowing climate change would affect their farm, the Ortmans decided to change their entire philosophy of farming. Instead of being a monoculture farm that just grew corn, they decided to grow a variety of organic crops. In addition to corn, they grow rye, soy, black beans, and strawberries. They also take meticulous care of their soil. Instead of using pesticides, they run tractors through their farms to scrape out the weeds. They work hard to cultivate compost, which they use on their soil. The compost is made out of manure and food waste products. It enriches the soil.

Soil is one of the most important aspects of the relationship between food and climate change. First, soil contains carbon. Earth's topsoil has 2,500 gigatons of carbon. (One gigaton equals 1 billion tons.) Deforestation and plowing has caused the soil to emit carbon back into the atmosphere. About half of the land where plants can grow has been used for agriculture (rangelands, pastures, and farms). Because of this, the soil has lost about 50 to 70 percent of its carbon to the air. According to the website Carbon Counts, soil's carbon is responsible for about a quarter of all man-made greenhouse gases. Therefore, in protecting soil, we are both protecting our food supply and limiting carbon emissions.

The second important thing about soil is that it is part of the water cycle. Soil stores 60 percent of rainfall. The Ortmans are smart to use compost and to not till their soil too often because plants growing in higher-quality soil actually need less water to grow into the vegetables and fruits that we need to eat.

The Ortmans think of themselves not as owners, but as stewards of the land. They are a family-run farm where every member of the family has different jobs. They work from sunup to sundown protecting this valuable and often overlooked aspect of our world: dirt. They know that in providing organic, diverse crops, they are helping protect this land and our food for future generations.

This is just one example of the intersection of climate change and food and water supplies. Throughout this book, we will be examining other intersections of our changing planet with a threatened food and water supply. First, we will look at exactly why and how climate change is affecting the food and water that we need to survive.

Shown here is Shanghai's Hongqiao Rail Station. The crowds of people at this and other transportation hubs around the world demonstrate the planet's growing population.

CHAPTER 1

The Impact of Climate Change on Food and Water Supplies

In a 2016 journal article, Shilu Tong and other authors state, "Climate change's most profound impacts are likely to be on food, health systems and water." This paper specifically looks at China. With a population of 1.4 billion people, China represents about 18 percent of the world's population. This is a lot of people to feed. Tong points out that climate change will adversely affect the Chinese population because of diminished food and water supplies. Let's take a look at the reasons why China, among other countries, will be severely affected by a changing climate.

Here is a blast furnace in Pennsylvania from the Industrial Revolution.

Rising Temperatures

First, Earth's temperature is rising. Global warming is thought to be anthropogenic, or caused by humans. Since the Industrial Revolution, humans have burned fossil fuels to create energy. Fossil fuels are commodities like oil, coal, and gas that put carbon dioxide into the atmosphere. Because of this, Earth's surface and ocean temperatures have risen. In 2018, Earth's temperature was 1.8 degrees Fahrenheit (1 degree Celsius) warmer than it was in 1800. This means that farmers in the 1800s grew food under very different weather patterns than modern farmers, like the Ortmans, do today. Today's farmers exist in a world that is heating up. There are more floods and more heat waves. Rain, a key component of creating a sustainable farm, fluctuates. When there is a deluge of water, the soil cannot soak it up. Then, there are periods of no water at all.

Greenhouse Gases

Global warming is connected to the greenhouse effect. The greenhouse effect is the process in which infrared radiation—invisible frequencies of the sun's light and heat—is absorbed by certain gases in the atmosphere, called greenhouse gases (GHGs), and reradiated down to Earth. The process works like a greenhouse, which is built to trap the sun's heat. In short, greenhouse gases warm the planet by trapping heat from the sun.

Greenhouse gases are extremely important. Without them, Earth would be an uninhabitable, frozen wasteland. Global surface temperatures would average 0°F (–18°C). Conversely, with too high a quantity of greenhouse gases, Earth would be like Venus, where the average surface temperature is 860°F (460°C). Until relatively recently, Earth's atmosphere contained the ideal level of greenhouse gases necessary for life. The main greenhouse gases in Earth's atmosphere are water vapor (H_2O), carbon dioxide (CO_2), methane (CH_4), nitrous oxide (N_2O), and ozone (O_3). Other gases, such as chlorofluorocarbons (CFCs), are also present, but in small percentages. Some greenhouse

Landfills emit methane.

gases occur naturally. Carbon dioxide is produced when humans and animals exhale. It is then absorbed by plants, which require it for photosynthesis and then emit oxygen as a waste product of the process. Volcanic eruptions can also release carbon dioxide from melted rocks deep inside the planet. Methane is created through many different natural processes in low-oxygen environments, like swamps, rivers, and even the digestive tracts of animals. Water vapor is simply the gas phase of water.

Certain human activities create greenhouse gases too. Landfills and grazing livestock, such as cows, emit methane. Nitrous oxide enters waterways and the atmosphere from fertilizers. Deforestation prevents carbon dioxide absorption by trees, resulting in a buildup of the gas in the atmosphere. Chlorofluorocarbons are used in refrigeration and in aerosol cans, and they are released into the air with each spray or after leaks. However, humanity's largest source of greenhouse gas emissions, by far, is the carbon dioxide emitted when fossil fuels—like oil, coal, and natural gas—are burned.

Fossil Fuels

As mentioned previously, humans burn fossil fuels like oil, natural gas, and coal for energy. We use that energy for transportation; to power industry; and to provide heat, air conditioning, and electricity to homes and businesses. Fossil fuels are formed from organisms that lived hundreds of millions of years ago, even before the first dinosaurs. When those organisms (plants, animals, and bacteria) died, they were buried under layers of rock, soil, and water. They then decomposed into simpler forms of organic material, becoming fossil fuels.

When they are burned, fossil fuels release lots of energy, and they also release lots of carbon dioxide. It enters the atmosphere and contributes to global warming more than any other greenhouse gas. For this reason, scientists talk about all greenhouse gases based on their equivalent in carbon dioxide.

Humans have been burning fossil fuels for thousands of years, but not in significant amounts until the Industrial Revolution. This was a period of enormous technological advances in

Here is a steam-powered switch engine from around 1887, the time of the Industrial Revolution.

agriculture, mining, transportation, textiles, manufacturing, and infrastructure that affected almost every aspect of daily life. Steam power paved the way. Steam engines, used in machinery and transportation, burned coal to boil water and create the steam that powered their mechanisms. This marked the beginning of humanity's ever-growing dependence on fossil fuels. Since the start of the Industrial Revolution, 500 gigatons of CO_2 have been emitted into the atmosphere, where it lingers for a very long time, absorbing more and more heat.

However, climate change is not a new or recent phenomenon. Earth's climate has changed several times throughout history, even before the Industrial Revolution and the sharp increase in carbon emissions into the atmosphere. According to the National

Aeronautics and Space Administration (NASA), there have been seven cycles of climate change in the last 650,000 years. There are many possible natural causes for these cycles, like changes in the sun's intensity, variations in Earth's orbit, and plate tectonics.

If Earth's climate has always been changing, since even before the Industrial Revolution, how do we know humans are to blame for this most recent period of climate change? We know human activity is driving the current warming of the planet and resulting climate change because Earth is getting warmer far more quickly than at any other time in the past 1,300 years. In fact, the warmest years on record have all occurred since 1998. Meanwhile, during the twentieth century, the global sea level rose 5.5 inches (14 centimeters) due to melting glaciers and ice caps, a rate of increase that was faster than in the previous twenty-seven centuries.

At the same time, we're burning more fossil fuels than ever. According to the World Bank, yearly carbon emissions increased by about 60 percent between 1990 and 2013, an alarming acceleration. There is a greater abundance of carbon dioxide in the atmosphere now than at any point in the past 800,000 years. Methane is at its highest level in 400,000 years. The climate change that is now occurring is entirely consistent with the way humans are treating the environment. It is the direct consequence of our modern, industrialized lifestyles.

COFFEE FARMS IN HONDURAS

Pickers collect coffee beans from a farm in Honduras in 2019.

In 2019 in Corquín, Honduras, a coffee farmer, Fredi Onan Vicen Peña, looked at his heat-sick farm with despair. His two brothers and one sister used to farm in Honduras, but in 2018, they moved to the United States to find better weather. Central America is a region in the world that is deeply impacted by climate change. Farming has become very difficult in this region. Changing rain patterns have not only made the water supply unpredictable but have also allowed pests to infiltrate the coffee crops. Agriculture is such a large source of income for Central Americans that they feel the impacts severely when their farms are not profitable.

Researchers estimate that climate change could cause 1.4 million people to leave Mexico and Central America by 2050. According to a 2019 *New York Times* article, 28 percent of Hondurans work in the agricultural industry. Some will leave to search for better weather, better soil, and better farming opportunities in the United States. In Corquín, Peña was left with a difficult decision. Should he abandon his farm or continue, hoping that weather will get better?

The effects of this situation are not isolated to Honduras. The coffee your family drinks often comes from Central America. If there are not farms left to grow the product, the supply in the United States and many other countries will be affected. We are global citizens, and we must remember that even a place that seems far away is interconnected with our own communities.

The Impact on Food

Climate change will seriously impact agriculture. Crops need specific weather conditions in order to survive. In the future, global temperatures, precipitation, pollution, and severe weather events will determine whether or not we'll be able to produce enough food for the growing population.

Different regions will be affected differently. For example, the northern regions of the United States will become wetter, while southern areas, especially the Southwest, will become even drier than they already are. Certain areas will get too hot and dry for crop production and will be prone to more frequent and devastating wildfires.

Agriculture all around the world will be disrupted by severe weather events, like droughts, heat waves, and floods. These severe weather events will be more frequent and intense than ever before.

The Impact on Fresh Water

Water is all around us. It's in the beverages we drink and the food we eat. Water is used to manufacture goods, irrigate crops, cool power plants, and create electricity. It's in the sky, and it's underground. It's even inside of the human body. Water is present in so many areas of our lives that we take it for granted. It may seem like we have plenty, but of all the water on Earth, 97 percent is undrinkable salt water. Less than 3 percent is fresh water, and two-thirds of that is frozen in glaciers and ice caps. In many parts of the world, water is scarce. Climate change is aggravating the issue, threatening our access to the clean water we need.

Hotter temperatures accelerate ice melt and water evaporation into the atmosphere. That extra water vapor is a greenhouse gas, and it warms Earth even more. Water vapor turns into precipitation (rain, snow, or hail), so more atmospheric water vapor means more precipitation. Over the past fifty years, rainfall has increased in the Northeast and Midwest of the United States. Storms are shifting northward, so rainfall in the Southeast and West has actually decreased. All around the world, precipitation has changed in frequency, location, and intensity. In the future, floods and droughts will be more frequent and severe. We'll see too little water in some places and too much in others. Some places could even see both floods and droughts at different times of the year.

Water quality is very sensitive to fluctuations in temperature and rainfall. Increased rainfall can actually increase water pollution by washing more pollutants from land surfaces into waterways. Floods can overload wastewater systems. Rising oceans may intrude on groundwater supplies (water pumped up from underground) and make them too salty to drink or use. Contaminated water supplies mean there is less to drink and use for crops.

The world's population grows every day. Water will be a key issue in global politics in the future. Conflict, some of it violent, will grow over dwindling water supplies.

Although climate change has a direct connection to food and water supplies, we must not give up hope. Survival is often about adapting to adverse conditions, as well as mitigating the situation, or making it less problematic. There are many ways that we can adjust our agriculture and our water usage so that we may still be able to live, perhaps in a different way, as Earth's climate changes.

Cover crops grown at this sustainable palm oil plantation in Southeast Asia protect the soil from erosion.

CHAPTER 2

Adaptation and Mitigation

NASA's Global Climate Change website proposes two types of strategies as a response to climate change. The first is mitigation. Mitigation means making something less painful. To mitigate climate change, we need to employ solutions that lower the amount of carbon emitted into the air. The second approach, adaptation, is a strategy that requires humans to be flexible and respond to the changing climate. This may require employing farming techniques or methods of obtaining and using water that we have never used before. The Ortmans adapted to climate change by growing a more diverse range of crops. In the words of Sherilyn Ortman, "[It's] better to embrace change on your own terms than wait until it embraces you by force."

Food Variety Extinction

Most of us have heard something about plant and animal extinctions in rain forests around the world. Very few of us, however, know anything about food variety extinction. Food varieties are becoming extinct. For instance, 86 percent of US apple varieties are gone. Over the course of human history, farmers selectively bred crops and livestock that were particularly suited to their local climate. However, after the Green Revolution that began in the mid-twentieth century, farmers favored a small number of high-yield, genetically enhanced species. Today, farmers all around the world rely on the same few breeds of crops and livestock. The desire for increased production has doomed many local varieties to extinction, decreasing biodiversity. Internationally, 75 percent of farmed plant diversity has disappeared.

That's a problem. The crops and livestock that we rely upon were genetically enhanced for one thing: greater yields. To survive in as many different climates as possible, the crops require expensive pesticides and fertilizers, while the livestock must consume special feed. High-yield varieties are weaker than varieties that have not been bred for high yields. They may lack the proper genes and immunities to survive climate change or disease.

For example, in 1999, *Puccinia graminis*, a fungus also called stem rust, spread around the world. In 2016, another variety of stem rust spread, hitting Italy especially hard. The stem rust, if left untreated, kills crops completely. In 2016, the fungus contaminated a significant area of land on the Italian island of Sicily. Researchers from the International Center for Agricultural Research in the Dry Areas (among other institutions) quickly trained people to control the outbreak so the spread would not become an epidemic.

Here is an up-close photograph of stem rust on wheat.

THE CHESAPEAKE BAY

Oysters are sustainably farmed in the Chesapeake Bay.

Chip Bowling is a farmer from the Chesapeake Bay watershed in Maryland. He has said, "If our fields are healthy, then the rivers are healthy, and aquatic life is healthy." Bowling sees all parts of his greater ecosystem as being connected. Oysters are a very valuable part of the water cycle. They can filter 50 gallons (190 liters) of water in one day. He wants to make sure that his fields allow the oysters in the surrounding area to remain healthy, so Bowling takes great care in planting so that he protects the soil of his farm. He uses cover crops. Cover crops are grasses and legumes that help protect the soil from eroding or becoming too compact. They also make the soil more nutrient rich. When Bowling is done harvesting for the season, he even leaves field edges behind so that animals will have a place to live. Bowling cares not only for his farm but also for the health of the greater ecosystem. He hopes his farm will attract a diverse range of animal species.

Climate change and disease will continue to threaten our food sources. Food biodiversity is a safety net. For example, there may be a local species of wheat that's immune to stem rust. Hopefully, we haven't let that species go extinct.

Farming Pollution

Just as climate change affects agriculture, agriculture affects climate change. Agriculture contributes to climate change by releasing CO_2 through deforestation, methane from rice cultivation and manure, and nitrous oxide from fertilizers. It also pollutes water supplies.

We can't simply write off conventional, high-yield farming practices, however. They have degraded the environment and contributed to climate change, but they've also saved billions of people from starving. Alternative farming practices may pollute less, but they typically produce smaller yields.

There are no simple solutions for ending world hunger. It is clear that we need to minimize our impact on the environment. Climate change will cause drought and famine. We need as much food as possible, but if we continue to pollute for short-term gain, we'll only hurt our chances of future survival.

Water Pollution

When we think of water pollution, most of us imagine major oil spills or factories spewing waste into rivers. Actually, most water pollution is caused by nonpoint sources, or sources that pollute indirectly. Runoff, for example, occurs when excess water, like rainfall, flows over the land. That runoff carries pollutants on the ground, like oil slicks, pesticides, or fertilizers, into waterways. Agricultural runoff has become the biggest source of water pollution in America. In the United States, livestock produce an incredible amount of manure each year. Harmful bacteria, viruses, and parasites from manure seep into underground waterways and are washed into rivers by runoff. Almost twenty million Americans are sickened every year from drinking contaminated water.

Manure also contains phosphorus and nitrogen from cattle feed and supplements, which chemically alter and damage aquatic ecosystems. When they leak into waterways, these substances can actually fertilize algae. The algae bloom, die, and suck the oxygen out of the water. These oxygen-deprived areas are known as dead zones because no organism can survive within them. Dead zones have already appeared at the mouths of most major rivers. Where the Mississippi River empties into the Gulf of Mexico, there's a dead zone the size of New Jersey.

Climate change will only make pollution worse. Increased rainfall intensity will cause more runoff. The US Environmental Protection Agency (EPA) expects that more waterways will be considered "impaired" in the future. That means fewer fish to eat, less water to drink, and more disease.

Changing Attitudes

Within the agricultural industry, there is a balance between being profitable and being true to a greater ideal. Many of the farmers we have talked about so far have struck this balance. They have not only found more sustainable food sources but also more economical ones.

A couple buys fresh vegetables at a farmers' market.

CHAPTER 3

Protecting Our Food and Water

Within our communities, there are businesses and government agencies. Together, we can create a meaningful dialogue between these two entities to encourage useful action. We can protect the food and water supplies that we have through government programs and private action. Solving the food crisis will take a multilayered approach. Both large-scale policy and smaller actions by individuals are needed to protect the environment. Working together is the only way that we will protect the food that has taken so many precious resources to grow.

Government Protection

The US Environmental Protection Agency is a governmental agency responsible for protecting the environment and human health by creating regulations and enforcing them. The EPA's regulations attempt to limit the negative impact an individual or business can have on the environment. For example, the EPA

Businesses like bakeries throw out a lot of perfectly fine food. The SMM Food Recovery Challenge was created to help divert this waste.

enforces a certain standard of air and water quality in an effort to prevent excessive pollution. In doing so, EPA regulations also help limit the human contribution to climate change.

One part of the EPA is the Sustainable Materials Management program (SMM). The SMM tries to lower the environmental impact of materials in their life cycle. The SMM looks at how materials are produced, how they are being used, and how they may be reused or recycled. In 2017, the SMM held a Food Recovery Challenge for businesses. It invited businesses to compete with each other to see who could divert the most food from landfills and incinerators. This might include producing less food or taking food that is not being sold and giving it to homeless shelters. Over one thousand participants helped reduce food waste. Together, they saved 648,000 tons (587,850 metric tons) of food from the landfill. This reduced carbon emissions by 493,835 tons (448,000 metric tons) of CO_2 equivalent. This is the same level of carbon reduction as taking ninety-six thousand cars off the road for one year.

In 2017, President Donald Trump wanted to cut funding for the EPA and to cut programs like the Food Recovery Challenge. Senator Chuck Schumer, from New York, spoke out against this, saying, "For the sake of our planet and the future of America, I will do everything in my power to protect the EPA from these disastrous cuts." The EPA serves an important and critical role in both educating people about and actively fixing problems associated with food.

Renewable Energy

Renewable energy comes from resources that are naturally replenished, like wind, water, or the sun. Fossil fuels, on the other hand, cannot be naturally replenished—once they're gone, they're gone. In this way, renewable energy sources can protect us from unexpected energy shortages or rising oil prices. Certain renewable energy sources are also considered clean because they don't release greenhouse gases into the atmosphere or contribute to global warming. Solar energy and wind power are both examples of clean, renewable energy sources.

Currently, renewable energy sources account for about 12.5 percent of the world's supply. We don't use more renewable energy because renewable energy plants are expensive to build and maintain in the short term. They also usually have to be in geographically remote locations where the energy source and space are most abundant. For example, solar power plants are often built in deserts, where sunlight is both reliable and plentiful. Because the plants are often far from the communities they serve, electricity transmission lines must be built over long distances.

In the future, however, we will use more renewable energy. The US Energy Information Administration projects that by 2050, 18 percent of the world's energy will come from renewable sources. Thanks to tax credits and government initiatives that encourage renewable energy projects, costs are driven down. Most people agree on the long-term benefits of renewable

SVALBARD GLOBAL SEED VAULT

In 2008, the Norwegian government opened the Svalbard Global Seed Vault in order to store seeds in case future generations lose their supply of seeds because of war or environmental disaster. People from all over the world shipped seeds there to be stored. The vault, built into the side of a mountain, is about 800 miles (1,300 kilometers) north of the Arctic Circle. It is a perfect place to store the seeds because the seeds can be kept very cold. They are kept at 0°F (–18°C). If the power were to go off, the seeds would still be safe, as the mountain naturally keeps the vault at between 21°F and 23°F (–6°C to –5°C). This is the largest collection of seeds in the world. The Ministry of Food and Agriculture of Norway understands the importance of protecting a diverse range of seeds for future generations.

The Svalbard Global Seed Vault sits in cold land north of the Arctic Circle.

energy, if only to promote energy independence (not having to rely on other countries for fuel supplies). Climate change and shrinking supplies of fossil fuels will force the issue. There's enormous potential for clean renewable resources to support our energy needs in the future. A happy by-product of greater reliance upon renewable energy sources will be food and water supplies untainted by toxins. Natural gas and coal taint the air and water. People experience breathing problems, heart attacks, and neurological damage, among other symptoms, when the air and water is contaminated. Renewable energy, like wind and solar power, does not pollute the air. Additionally, wind and solar energy require no water and therefore do not affect the water supply.

Water Consumption

Even though the US population has grown, water consumption hasn't increased correspondingly in the past few years. That's all due to new technology, new laws, and public awareness campaigns. Even so, Americans still use too much water—about twice as much as the world's average. On average, Americans use 80 to 100 gallons (302 to 378 L) of water per day. The most water is used when flushing toilets and taking showers and baths. Many state governments will offer individuals a tax credit if they put in a toilet that uses less water or sink faucets that have a lower flow of water.

At this point, the best way to protect our water supply is to use less. Engineering can help us in this effort. There are some new technologies and methods that are making it even easier to conserve water. Some people use gray water—wastewater from household activities like dishwashing, bathing, or laundry that can be recycled for use on lawns or gardens or to flush toilets. Gray water doesn't contain any human waste, but it isn't clean enough to drink. New, specially designed plumbing systems can collect and store gray water in homes and businesses. Gray water relieves the growing pressure on water systems by reducing freshwater demand and usage and decreasing the amount of water flowing to treatment plants.

Rain barrels, or rainwater tanks, also help conserve water by collecting and storing rainfall and runoff. That water can be used to water gardens, flush toilets, or even for drinking if it's properly filtered and cleaned. It might seem like it would be a time-consuming and expensive undertaking to buy and install a rain barrel, but many people use small, inexpensive containers to collect rain. Even something as humble and basic as empty milk jugs, for example, can effectively harvest rain. Suburbanites and urban gardeners are increasingly using specially designed rain barrels that are covered and are attached by hosing to storm gutters. Meanwhile, many people use open rain barrels in rural areas around the world. The downside is that these improvised, coverless rain barrels collect less water and are vulnerable to bugs that lay eggs in standing water, like mosquitoes.

Rain barrels are a great way to collect and recycle water.

The turf grass that is used on lawns across America is the largest irrigated crop in the United States. Given the amount of water and chemical fertilizer needed to maintain a green lawn in the heat of summer, it seems increasingly unnecessary and ecologically irresponsible to waste precious resources and introduce chemicals into the soil and water table just for the sake of a decorative plot of green grass. Xeriscape landscapes are designed to reduce or eliminate the need for irrigation. They use planning, soil analysis, plant selection, and efficient irrigation to promote water conservation and prevent pollution. Xeriscape landscapes also take less time and effort to maintain. They're promoted in over forty states, especially in regions that don't have access to reliable water sources, like the American Southwest. Using gray water and rain barrels can also help limit the enormously wasteful impact of watering lawns.

Preparing for Tomorrow

As you can see, when people come together and share their ideas, good things happen. Food and water sources are being protected by a variety of groups: businesses, governments, and ordinary citizens. However, new solutions for how we grow food and live our lives must also be implemented if we are going to be able to feed our growing population.

Poplar trees, like these in Germany, grow rapidly and therefore consume a lot of carbon dioxide.

CHAPTER 4

New Solutions

Many times, dire situations lead to innovative solutions. Engineers, architects, and farmers are rethinking how food is grown. They are even rethinking concepts like "sunlight," "trees," and "land." By challenging the traditional modes of thinking, these innovators are allowing humans to mitigate global warming and adapt to the strain that climate change places on food sources.

Inventions and Innovations

Engineers have invented "artificial trees," structures that absorb carbon dioxide just like a tree does. These structures use a special resin to which carbon clings. The resin can then release the CO_2 for storage under controlled conditions, preventing it from staying in the atmosphere and trapping the sun's heat. The captured CO_2 can be sold to businesses that need it, like soda companies or greenhouses. This technology already exists, but it's not yet cost effective. As the need grows and demand for such a solution increases, the cost will probably come down as the volume of artificial tree production climbs.

What if we could reflect heat from the sun back into space? Some scientists have suggested building a giant screen of crisscrossed aluminum strands. The screen would be carried into space by a rocket or spacecraft and released. Once situated, it would repel infrared radiation, but not completely keep the sun's light and heat from reaching Earth. It would be an extremely difficult undertaking, considering how big the screen would need to be and how challenging its design, construction, placement, and maintenance would be. Using the same principle, however, we could also try a more earthbound approach. Icy regions around the world could be blanketed with reflectors. Certain specially designed blankets are already used in the Alps to protect ski hills from melting in the summer. This would be a large-scale version of that practice, designed to reflect the sun's heat away from the planetary surface.

Reforestation is a great way to remove and absorb carbon from the atmosphere and limit habitat loss from deforestation, but it can be a time-consuming and expensive process. Why plant one tree at a time when you can just drop a "seed bomb"? Seeds packed in biodegradable material can be dropped from

VERTICAL FARMING

In an old laser tag facility in Newark, New Jersey, lettuce grows. There is no sunlight. There is not even any dirt. From the outside, AeroFarms looks like an abandoned warehouse. Inside, though, there are vertical farms that are 30 feet (9 meters) tall. The inventor of this system realized that plants don't need soil or water immersion to grow, but rather mist. They mist the plants with nutrients and give them artificial light. This allows the lettuce to grow without any herbicides or pesticides, and it cuts the growing cycle in half. In addition, while runoff from traditional farming contaminates freshwater sources, AeroFarms' indoor system does not contaminate local waterways. It has a small impact on the environment and provides fresh greens for people to eat all year long.

The AeroFarms facility in Newark is pictured here.

airplanes in large numbers, allowing them to be dispersed across a wide area. This could become a much quicker, easier, cheaper, more efficient, and less labor-intensive way to plant trees and create huge carbon sinks.

Crops and Climate Change

Experts are trying to invent new ways to protect the world's food supplies and maximize future production, all while limiting agriculture's impact on the environment. For example, scientists are working hard to develop climate change–resistant crops. These crops would be better suited to the higher temperatures and variable precipitation expected in the future. That way, food production wouldn't drop off drastically, even if the consequences of climate change are as harsh as some computer models suggest.

South Africa is one country that is using biotechnology to create crops that are drought-resistant and that can survive even when the soil is not fertile. The first genetically modified crop, maize, was used in South Africa in 1996. By 2001, the country was growing maize, cotton, and soybeans this way. In 2017, South Africa converted 6.7 million acres (2.7 million hectares) of land for its genetically modified crops. The crop production was so great in South Africa that farmers began to export their crops. Previously, they had only enough for their own country's supply.

South Africa is just one example of a country that is using biotechnology to its advantage. The United States, Brazil, and

Above is a field of wheat in South Africa, where many farmers are rethinking their crops.

India are among the top users of genetically modified crops in the world.

Cloning

Someday, you might drink milk from a cloned cow. Cloning is very attractive because it gives farmers complete control over their livestock's genes. Through cloning, they could also enrich milk and meat with vitamins and nutrients, which would help solve the world's massive and persistent malnutrition problem. The US Food and Drug Administration (FDA), which sets standards for food quality, has already approved meat and milk from cloned cattle, pigs, and goats. According to the FDA, food from these cloned animals is just as safe as food from non-cloned ones.

Rethinking Agriculture

Another way in which farming may soon change is in its locale. So-called urban farms—mostly small plots of land reclaimed from abandoned city lots—have been growing in popularity in recent years. Urban farming may also soon be moving up in the world—way up. Vertical farming is urban agriculture at its most extreme. Many people believe that it's more efficient and environmentally responsible to farm inside of skyscrapers using green growing methods. That way, farmers can maximize the amount grown within a certain area of land—by growing upward rather than growing outward—while using energy-efficient and eco-friendly agricultural practices, including the elimination of toxic chemical runoff, water waste, and soil depletion.

Farms can be major producers of greenhouse gases, particularly methane. Cows contribute to climate change by releasing methane in their manure and flatulence (digestive gas). To fix that problem, some scientists have suggested feeding cows garlic. As strange as it sounds, garlic kills methane-producing bacteria in cows' stomachs, thereby cutting their greenhouse gas emissions!

Cloud Seeding

What if we could control the rain and generate precipitation whenever we needed to replenish our dwindling freshwater supplies? Far-fetched as it sounds, this might actually be possible. When silver iodide or dry ice (frozen carbon dioxide) particles are

Here is a diagram of two ways cloud seeding works: a plane or a ground generator disperses particles into the clouds to create rainfall.

dropped on clouds from above, precipitation increases, possibly by 10 to 15 percent.

In January of 2019, the Korea Meteorological Administration (KMA) and the Ministry of Environment carried out attempts at cloud seeding over the Yellow Sea, but they were unsuccessful. A thin mist, rather than a heavy downpour, was generated. This wasn't the KMA's first attempt to produce rain unnaturally. They are very concerned about air pollution in South Korea and have been attempting to make it rain so that the water clears fine dust from the air. In 2017, the country spent $14.4 million to buy a cloud-seeding airplane. In 2018, they attempted cloud seeding twelve times. None of these attempts were successful.

Thirty-seven other countries have been attempting to produce rain with cloud seeding for various reasons. In 2011,

Here, people set up a cloud seeding rocket from the back of a truck.

China tried to use cloud seeding to increase its agriculture, specifically its grain harvest. However, none of these attempts have been very successful. Cloud seeding theoretically seems like a useful idea, but in actuality it may still be beyond our reach.

Desalination

We're running low on water, so why not turn to the vast water resources surrounding every continent? Desalination is a process whereby salt and other minerals are removed from ocean water to make it drinkable. There are two methods to desalinate water. One is distillation, where water is boiled so that the water vapors are collected but the salt is left behind. The second method is reverse osmosis, where water is forced through a membrane which removes the salt.

At first glance, it may seem like it would solve all of our water supply problems, but desalination accounted for only 1 percent of global water usage as of 2015. Why? It's not suited for inland or high-altitude areas that are far from oceans and that would require long-distance transport of the desalinated water. Also, it's expensive, since desalination requires enormous amounts of energy to function. In addition, if that energy is produced by fossil fuels, desalination will contribute to climate change. This is the case in the Middle East, where desalination may seem like a logical way to expand the region's limited freshwater resources. However, two-thirds of the desalinated water for the Middle East is distilled using heat created by burning fossil fuels. The other third is made through reverse osmosis, which requires electricity, and much of that electricity also comes from burning fossil fuels. Desalination technology is improving, however, and there is the potential to use renewable energy sources to desalinate water in the future. That would prevent emissions and make desalination cheaper in the long run.

You may disagree with some of the solutions to the food and water emergency. You may wonder why humans are creating many unnatural solutions to this dilemma. Perhaps it would be better for all of us to cut down our carbon emissions than to use science and technology to create human-made solutions. If you feel this way, there are many options for activism and habit change that you can explore. Ordinary people, both kids and adults, can be environmental advocates and leaders.

Commuting by bicycle is very popular in Amsterdam.

CHAPTER 5

Change Yourself, Change the World

We can all do our part to help adapt to and mitigate the effects of climate change. It takes conscious decisions to change your habits, but each day's decisions may result in an entirely new eco-friendly lifestyle. You may find that the following suggestions are not only environmentally beneficial but also fun and economically beneficial as well.

New Habits

One of the best ways to limit your impact on the environment is to conserve nonrenewable resources by reducing consumption. Do your best to use less water, less energy, and fewer packaged goods. It's all interconnected—power plants use water, water

Consider refilling your own water bottle rather than buying water in disposable plastic bottles.

treatment facilities use electricity, and manufacturers use both water and electricity.

It's easy to conserve water. Turn off the tap when you're brushing your teeth or washing dishes. Take showers instead of baths, and make them quick. If you notice a leaky faucet, tell your parents and get it fixed. Leaks can account for 10,000 gallons (37,854 L) of wasted water every year. That's enough to fill a swimming pool.

Don't use bottled water unless you have to. Bottled water is much more expensive and generates lots of plastic waste. Try a water filter or filtered pitcher instead—they're cheap ways to make sure that your water is clean. If you have to buy bottled water, buy big bottles to limit your trash. Reusable containers are always better than disposable. A thermos or aluminum water bottle, for example, is a great, permanent alternative to disposable plastic bottles.

LED light bulbs are pictured here.

When you have trash, recycle what you can. There are recycling programs all around the country that collect certain materials in trash so they can be reused. Sort your aluminum, plastic, and paper goods. The symbol of three arrows chasing one another in a triangle shows that something is recyclable or made of recycled materials, but it doesn't necessarily mean you can recycle it in your area. Different cities have different rules. Check your hometown's recycling and sanitation website for information.

Conserving electricity will limit water usage and the amount of fossil fuels your local power plant burns. Turn off lights and electronics when you don't need them. Plugged-in appliances, especially those with electronic displays or clocks, actually drain small amounts of electricity even when they're turned off, so if you go on a trip, unplug your appliances. Replace your light bulbs with new, more energy-efficient LED ones.

Meanwhile, changing your transportation habits can lower your reliance on fossil fuels and reduce your carbon footprint. You can save gasoline by walking, riding your bike, carpooling, or taking public transportation whenever possible.

Organic Food

You've most likely seen organic food in your supermarket. What does "organic" mean? According to the US Department of Agriculture (USDA), "Organic is a labeling term that indicates that the food or other agricultural product has been produced through approved methods that integrate cultural, biological, and mechanical practices that foster cycling of resources, promote ecological balance, and conserve biodiversity." That means

B CORP COMPANIES

Some companies—known as B Corp companies—are redefining what it means to be a responsible business. Instead of just looking at how much money they make, they are also thinking about their environmental and societal impact. Companies have to have their entire business reviewed in order to be qualified as a B Corp. The certification was held by only about 2,800 companies around the world as of 2019.

Next time you need to buy something, think about buying it from a B Corp company. Patagonia is an example of a company in the United States that is B Corp certified. The company cares about the environmental impact its products are having, and it fights for protection of wild spaces. Spending money on products from a company like this one is one way to do your part to help the environment.

no genetic enhancements, synthetic fertilizers, hormones, or chemical pesticides or herbicides.

It's important to know how your food is grown and where it comes from. Most fruits and vegetables are packaged and shipped over long distances before they reach your shelf. Delivery trucks and cargo ships burn fossil fuels and release greenhouse gases into the atmosphere. It's best to buy from local, sustainable, small-scale farmers who care about their environmental impact. Their produce, meat, and eggs may be slightly more expensive, but your money will support a local, responsible business, not a corporation concerned more about profit than about food quality, consumer safety, and environmental protection and sustainability. Check the labels next time you're in the grocery store.

Eat Less Meat

Eating less meat is another way to help the environment. Livestock require large amounts of food and water, not to mention grazing land cleared of trees—all of which stress the environment. If you do eat meat, try to get it from an environmentally conscious farm, one that not only uses sound ecological practices but also uses grass feed and does not inject its cows with hormones.

Use Ecosia

Consider using Ecosia as your go-to search engine. This website uses its profits to plant trees every time you search. They plant trees in places that need them the most: Africa, South America, and Asia. The site is very progressive about the environment. It is completely carbon neutral, and every search removes 2.2 pounds (1 kilogram) of carbon dioxide from the air. In 2017, the search engine built its own solar energy plant. If Ecosia were as popular as Google, we would be able to remove 15 percent of carbon emissions.

Urban Gardening

If you're interested, you can learn more about growing food. There are many community gardens and co-ops that provide classes. Learning about where food comes from is a great way to stay healthy and prepare for climate change. If you live in a city, there are plenty of urban agricultural organizations, rooftop gardens, and greenhouses sprouting up all around the country that are great places to start learning more about the land and how to care for it. If you want to do more, help plant trees locally

Consider eating less meat, like this vegetarian Indian food.

and consider growing your own vegetable garden or joining a community garden.

Be an Informed Citizen

Find out more about the area you live in. What type of power plant generates your electricity? How old is your water system? How clean is your water? Does your city allow gray water systems? Where does your food come from? The more you know, the more informed your decision-making can be about how to create a more sustainable life. Look for local environmental organizations to join, volunteer for, or donate to. If you disagree with local, state, or national policies, write to your mayor, state representative, or senator.

Stewards of the Land

The Ortman family follows this quote from Chief Seattle: "We do not inherit the earth from our ancestors; we borrow it from our children." They believe that, as farmers, they are stewards, or protectors, of the land. Food and water shortages are a serious problem for the twenty-first century. We each must think of ourselves as stewards of our Earth. Although we cannot quickly find a solution to global warming, we can make small changes that will create a better and more environmentally conscious culture. This will benefit not only us but future generations as well. The best thing we can do for the next generation is give them a healthier planet.

Glossary

adapt To adjust to changing circumstances or conditions and continue to flourish. In terms of climate change, to alter human behavior to respond to the negative effects of climate change.

anthropogenic Caused by humans.

biotechnology Technology that allows humans to alter living things to create products like medicines or drought-resistant crops.

carbon sink Something that collects and stores carbon, such as a forest or ocean.

climate change Lasting changes in temperature and weather patterns.

dead zone A low-oxygen area in a body of water where it is difficult to sustain fish and aquatic plant life.

fossil fuel A nonrenewable energy source like oil, coal, or natural gas that releases greenhouse gases, particularly carbon dioxide, when burned.

global warming The rising of average world surface and ocean temperatures.

gray water Recycled wastewater from household activities that can be used to water gardens and lawns and flush toilets.

greenhouse effect The process whereby radiation from the sun is trapped in the atmosphere by gases like carbon dioxide. At a normal level, this results in global surface temperatures warm enough to sustain life. At an elevated level, the greenhouse effect drives climate change.

Green Revolution The period of increased agricultural production, beginning in the 1940s, because of technological advances.

Industrial Revolution The period from the eighteenth through the nineteenth centuries during which technological advances transformed industry and daily life and resulted in the first large-scale emissions from fossil fuels.

mitigation The act of decreasing the impact of human activities that are resulting in global warming and climate change.

monoculture The cultivation of a single crop.

nonpoint sources Indirect sources of pollution.

organic food Food produced through natural methods, without synthetic pesticides, chemical fertilizers, hormones, or genetic modification.

renewable energy Energy from naturally replenished sources, such as wind, sunlight, and water.

sustainable Not depleting or permanently damaging a resource.

yield The amount of something produced, such as crops.

Further Information

Books

Brown, Gabe. *Dirt to Soil: One Family's Journey into Regenerative Agriculture.* White River Junction, VT: Chelsea Green Publishing, 2018.

Malizia, Diana. *A Visual Guide to Weather and Climate*. New York, NY: Rosen YA, 2018.

Mihaly, Christy, and Sue Heavenrich. *Diet for a Changing Climate: Food for Thought*. Minneapolis, MN: Twenty-First Century Books, 2019.

Scibilia, Jade Zora. *Climate Change*. New York, NY: PowerKids Press, 2019.

Wallace-Wells, David. *The Uninhabitable Earth*. New York, NY: Penguin Random House, 2019.

Websites

Green My Parents
http://greenmyparents.com
This website teaches kids how to think of green habit changes that save families money.

US Environmental Protection Agency
https://www.epa.gov/sustainable-management-food
Readers can learn about issues related to food and the environment. Students who work at jobs where food waste is a problem may consider asking their employers to join the Food Recovery Challenge.

Organizations

Charity: Water
40 Worth Street, Suite 330
New York, NY 10013
(646) 688-2323
Website: https://www.charitywater.org
Charity: Water brings clean, drinkable water to people in developing countries.

Miya
2 Rue de Bitbourg
L-1273 Hamm, Luxembourg
email: Info@miya-water.com
Website: http://www.miya-water.com/en
Miya helps create efficient uses of water in Africa, the Caribbean, and Europe.

Nature Canada
Suite 300, 75 Albert Street
Ottawa, ON, Canada
K1P 5E7
(800) 267-4088
Website: https://naturecanada.ca
Nature Canada is the oldest environmental organization in Canada. It helps preserve and protect parks and wildlife areas.

Svalbard Global Seed Vault
Postbox 8129 Dep, 0032
Oslo, Norway
email: redaksjonen@dss.dep.no
Website: https://www.regjeringen.no/en/topics/food-fisheries-and-agriculture/svalbard-global-seed-vault/id462220
The Svalbard Global Seed Vault aims to protect seeds for the future in case of a catastrophe.

Selected Bibliography

Ahrens, C. Donald, and Perry J. Samson. *Extreme Weather and Climate*. Belmont, CA: Brooks/Cole, 2010.

"Climate Change: How Do We Know?" NASA Global Climate Change. Accessed May 13, 2019. http://climate.nasa.gov/evidence.

Evans, Robert. "New Green Farming Vital to End Global Hunger." Reuters, July 5, 2011. http://www.reuters.com/article/2011/07/05/us-un-farms-idUSTRE7641MT20110705.

"Greenhouse - Green Planet." PBS: *Nova* Online. Accessed May 13, 2019. http://www.pbs.org/wgbh/nova/ice/greenhouse.html.

Jameson. "How Climate Change Impacts Soil Health - 2018." Climate Counts, August 5, 2018. https://www.climatecounts.org/environment/how-climate-change-impacts-soil-health.

Kosik, Alison. "Experts: U.S. Water Infrastructure in Trouble." CNN, January 21, 2011. http://www.cnn.com/2011/US/01/20/water.main.infrastructure/index.html.

Kunzig, Robert. "Population Seven Billion." *National Geographic* 219, no. 1 (January 2011): 32-69.

Quartz. "Future of Food: Farming in the Age of Climate Change." YouTube, November 22, 2017. https://www.youtube.com/watch?v=Tjr6z1GMDqc.

Semple, Kirk. "Central American Farmers Head to the U.S., Fleeing Climate Change." *New York Times*, April 13, 2019. https://www.nytimes.com/2019/04/13/world/americas/coffee-climate-change-migration.html.

Stories. "This Farm of the Future Uses No Soil and 95% Less Water." YouTube, July 5, 2016. https://www.youtube.com/watch?v=-_tvJtUHnmU.

"Svalbard Global Seed Vault." Norwegian Ministry of Agriculture and Food. Accessed April 30, 2019. https://www.regjeringen.no/en/topics/food-fisheries-and-agriculture/svalbard-global-seed-vault/id462220.

Index

About the Author

Alex David has her MFA from New England State College. She has written a series of books called *We the Weirdos*. Her poems and short stories have been published in literary journals such as *Green Mountains Review* and *Adelaide Literary Magazine*. Additionally, she has taught a class on eco-fiction at Canisius College in Buffalo, New York. She loves to learn and write about climate science. She is hopeful for the future.